CAMBRIDGE LIBRARY COLLECTION

Books of enduring scholarly value

Cambridge

The city of Cambridge received its royal charter in 1201, having already been home to Britons, Romans and Anglo-Saxons for many centuries. Cambridge University was founded soon afterwards and celebrates its octocentenary in 2009. This series explores the history and influence of Cambridge as a centre of science, learning, and discovery, its contributions to national and global politics and culture, and its inevitable controversies and scandals.

Ceremonies of the University of Cambridge

The formal ceremonies at Cambridge University can seem esoteric and baffling to newcomers and visitors. This 1926 publication answers questions including: what happens during the installation of the Chancellor of the University? What were the historical duties of the Proctors? When and why did the square cap worn by the undergraduate originate? Who are the Esquire Bedells, and what is the traditional order at Degree Congregations? H. P. Stokes attends in turn to the main topics surrounding Cambridge traditions, including points of etiquette, historical origins, important personnel and academic dress. Clearly organised for ease of reference, the book is also illustrated throughout with historical photographs.

T0384712

Cambridge University Press has long been a pioneer in the reissuing of out-of-print titles from its own backlist, producing digital reprints of books that are still sought after by scholars and students but could not be reprinted economically using traditional technology. The Cambridge Library Collection extends this activity to a wider range of books which are still of importance to researchers and professionals, either for the source material they contain, or as landmarks in the history of their academic discipline.

Drawing from the world-renowned collections in the Cambridge University Library, and guided by the advice of experts in each subject area, Cambridge University Press is using state-of-the-art scanning machines in its own Printing House to capture the content of each book selected for inclusion. The files are processed to give a consistently clear, crisp image, and the books finished to the high quality standard for which the Press is recognised around the world. The latest print-on-demand technology ensures that the books will remain available indefinitely, and that orders for single or multiple copies can quickly be supplied.

The Cambridge Library Collection will bring back to life books of enduring scholarly value across a wide range of disciplines in the humanities and social sciences and in science and technology.

Ceremonies of the University of Cambridge

H. P. STOKES

CAMBRIDGE
UNIVERSITY PRESS

CAMBRIDGE UNIVERSITY PRESS

Cambridge New York Melbourne Madrid Cape Town Singapore São Paolo Delhi

Published in the United States of America by Cambridge University Press, New York

www.cambridge.org
Information on this title: www.cambridge.org/9781108002325

© in this compilation Cambridge University Press 2009

This edition first published 1927
This digitally printed version 2009

ISBN 978-1-108-00232-5

This book reproduces the text of the original edition. The content and language reflect
the beliefs, practices and terminology of their time, and have not been updated.

CEREMONIES
OF THE UNIVERSITY
OF CAMBRIDGE

CAMBRIDGE
UNIVERSITY PRESS
LONDON: Fetter Lane

NEW YORK
The Macmillan Co.

BOMBAY, CALCUTTA and
MADRAS
Macmillan and Co., Ltd.

TORONTO
The Macmillan Co. of
Canada, Ltd.

TOKYO
Maruzen-Kabushiki-Kaisha

All rights reserved

*The
Chancellor's
Seal*

CEREMONIES
OF THE UNIVERSITY
OF CAMBRIDGE

by the

REV. H. P. STOKES
LL.D., LITT.D., F.S.A.

HON. FELLOW
OF CORPUS CHRISTI COLLEGE
HON. CANON OF ELY

CAMBRIDGE
AT THE UNIVERSITY PRESS
MCMXXVII

PRINTED IN GREAT BRITAIN

PREFATORY NOTE

ALTHOUGH this book takes some account of the changes brought about by the New Statutes, it reflects in the main the procedure prior to 1 October 1926.

The writer desires to express his obligations to the late Vice-Chancellor (Dr Seward, Master of Downing College), to the Rev. the Master of Corpus (Dr Pearce), to the Master of Christ's (Sir A. Shipley), to the late Registrary (Dr Keynes), to his successor (Mr E. Harrison), to the Senior Esquire Bedell (Mr R. Hamblin Smith), to Mr S. C. Roberts, to Mr S. Gaselee (for special help), and to the courteous officials at the various University buildings.

Indebtedness is also acknowledged to many former officials—Esquire Bedells and Registraries—who have left *memoranda*: notably to Matthew Stokes and to John Buck, whose MSS were printed by Dean Peacock in his *Observations*, etc. (1840). It is usual specially to mention Adam Wall, of Christ's, who in 1798 issued a volume on *University Ceremonies*, and Henry Gunning, who re-edited the same in 1828; but these writers failed to recognise their obligations to John Beverley, another member of the same college, who had already in 1788 published *An Account of the different Ceremonies observed in the Senate House,* etc.

An admirable article on the same subject was compiled by Dr Tanner, in that remarkable volume, *The Historical Register of the University of Cambridge.*

The writer is also indebted to *Country Life* for the loan of the block of the Vice-Chancellor's Rings.

H. P. S.

1926

CONTENTS

Prefatory Note   page   v

The Chancellor   1

The Vice-Chancellor   6

The Registrary   11

The Proctors   14

The Esquire Bedells   19

Matriculation   25

Congregations and Graces   27

   Supplicats   28

Degrees   29

   The Senior Wrangler, and the Wooden
     Spoon   31

   The Tripos   32

Commencement Day   36

Insignia Doctoralia   38

Honorary Degrees   40

University Costume   43

Processions   49

The Presentation of an Address to H.M.
   The King   53

The Bidding Prayer   page 54
University Sermons   56
The Orator   58
The High Steward   60
Representation in Parliament   61
The Commissary   63
University Discipline; the *Sex Viri*, etc.   64
H.M. Judges and Trinity College   66
The Admission of the newly elected
    Master of Trinity   67
Commemoration of Benefactors   69
The University and College Chests   71
Obsolete Officers   73
    The Master of Glomery   73
    The Master in Grammar   75
    Taxors   76
    Scrutators   76
    Gagers, Prisers, etc.   77
The University and Stourbridge Fair   78
The University Arms   80
The University Motto   81

Index   83

ILLUSTRATIONS

The Chancellor's Seal   *frontispiece*

From *The Seals and Armorial Insignia of the University and Colleges of Cambridge.* By W. H. St J. Hope

The Senate House   *facing p.* 5

As shown on the medals ſtruck at the inſtallation of the Duke of Northumberland as Chancellor in 1840

The Essex Cup   *facing p.* 6

From a photograph in the possession of Sir Arthur Shipley

The Vice-Chancellor's Rings   *facing p.* 8

From a photograph in the possession of Sir Arthur Shipley, firſt reproduced in *Country Life*

A Junior Proctor with his "bull-dogs"   *facing p.* 15

From a photograph of Mr H. G. Comber, D.S.O.

An Esquire Bedell (1815) with a Yeoman
Bedell   *facing p.* 20

From Ackermann's *Hiſtory of the University*

The Maces   *facing p.* 22

From a photograph in the possession of Sir Arthur Shipley

Admission of the Senior Wrangler in 1842 *facing p.* 31

From the drawing by R. B. Harraden

Presentation of the Wooden Spoon   *facing p.* 32

The laſt Wooden Spoon   *facing p.* 34
  By permission. From a photograph lent by A. W.
  Crisp and Co.

The University Cheſt   *facing p.* 72

The Taxors   *facing p.* 76
The Mayor and Corporation paying hom⁄
  age to the University Authorities
  From the Hare MS in the Regiſtry

The Arms and Motto of the University   *p.* 82

THE CHANCELLOR

THE CHANCELLOR has always ſtood firſt among the University officials. A liſt of those who have filled this diſtinguished poſt reaches back to the middle of the thirteenth century, and the office is mentioned familiarly quite early in that century. At firſt the Chancellors were elected annually, and this arrange⁄ ment held for some three hundred years; but at the beginning of the sixteenth century the celebrated Bishop John Fisher was continued in office for more than thirty years. Afterwards the practice was com⁄ menced of choosing some diſtinguished outsider; the Vice⁄Chancellor acting as the resident head of Uni⁄ versity affairs. It may be mentioned that of the firſt eight Chancellors thus chosen, six perished on the scaffold.

We need not here record the method of the election of the Chancellor, which may be read in Beverley (pp. 123⁄5); but it may be noted that, in the *Memoran⁄ dum* of the University Commissioners on the Proposed New Statutes made 29 January 1926, the firſt par⁄ ticular is "a method of nominating candidates for the office of Chancellor of the University."

Dealing as we do here with Ceremonies, we may at once proceed to refer to the installation of the Chancellor, which has generally taken place at the private residence of that great official, though it has usually been followed by some public function at Cambridge.

Take, as an example, the following description of the Manner of Installing our noble Chancellor the Earl of Holland, 29 October 1628, as recorded in *Buck's Book*:

About 9 of the clock in the morning, the University met at Southampton House, where they put on their formalities in the Hall, etc., when word was brought us that my Lord was ready, we ranked ourselves in this order: the Junior Bedel went before the Regents in their seniority, 2 and 2 together; then followed the non-Regents and Bachelors of Divinity, in the like manner; then the Taxers and after them the Proctors. The Senior Bedel went before the Vice-Chancellor. The Bishops followed him. Then came our University Doctors, in their scarlet gowns; and after them the Doctors of London, which had no scarlet.

When we were come to Warwick House, the Regents and non-Regents made a fair lane, by siding themselves in the court-yard, for our Chancellor, who came to meet the Vice-Chancellor, Bishops and Doctors, etc. When our Chancellor had given a courteous respect to all, he went up with the Vice-Chancellor next to him into the hall; the Bishops, Doctors and the rest did follow after.

There were 2 chairs placed at the upper end of the Hall, and also a little table before them to keep off the crowd. The Vice-Chancellor, standing before our Chancellor, did make his speech: about the middle of which, he willed the Senior Proctor to read the Patent: which being ended, the Vice-Chancellor delivered the same unto our Chancellor, together with the book of Statutes fairly bound up: and then spoke some things concerning them, etc. Then he went and sat down in the chair upon the left hand of our Chancellor; and, when he had taken his right hand in his own, the Senior Proctor gave him this oath, Domine, dabes Fidem in verbo Honoris, quod bene et fideliter Officium Cancellariatus Academiæ Cantabrigiensis præstabis.

Then they both rose up, and the Vice-Chancellor went to the table again, and in 3 or 4 lines ended his speech, telling his Honour, that our orator should supply his defects, in a better language.

Then the Orator began his speech; and when he had done, our Chancellor spake something very briefly and softly concerning the preservation of our Charters and Privileges, etc. Then he went up with the Vice-Chancellor and the Bishops and the rest of the Company into the Dining Room, where was a most sumptuous Dinner provided.

After dinner was over, our Chancellor came with the Vice-Chancellor and the rest of the Company as far as the court gate, where he very courteously parted with them. Mem. He stood bare all the time of both speeches.

The Vice-Chancellor caused one of the Bedels to give the servants which kept the gate at Warwick House 10s., and the porter at Southampton House 5s.

Detailed reports of similar functions in connection with succeeding Chancellors may be seen in Cooper's *Annals*; but we may pass to the following brief account of the installation of the present distinguished holder of the office:

On Oct. 29th, 1919, Mr A. J. Balfour [now the Earl of Balfour, K.G.] was inaugurated as Chancellor at 4 Carlton Gardens. The officials of the University journeyed to London, and reached the house at about 11.30 a.m.—the ceremony taking place in the Drawing Room at 12 noon. A procession was formed consisting of the Vice-Chancellor, the Registrary, the Public Orator, and the Proctors (each Proctor having one constable). On reaching the Drawing Room, which had been arranged on similar lines to the Senate House, the Vice-Chancellor took the Chair. The Senior Bedell then retired to escort the Chancellor Elect into the room; and the Junior Bedell

escorted the Vice-Chancellor to the door to receive the Chancellor Elect. The Bedells then escorted the Chancellor Elect to the chair—the Vice-Chancellor following. [Here follows the form of Procedure.]
  The Chancellor afterwards entertained the company to lunch. Robes were worn. The Senior Bedell wore the chain presented by the Chancellor Elect all through the ceremony. About 30 members of the Senate attended. Full academic dress was worn—Cap, Gown, Hood and Bands.

After the personal installation at his private residence, the new Chancellor generally pays a formal visit to the University, elaborate functions and entertainments being held, and calls being made at the various colleges. At the special gathering in the Senate House, honorary degrees are conferred, and an ode composed for the occasion is generally performed. The classic instance is that of 1 July 1760 at the installation of the Duke of Grafton as Chancellor, when the celebrated ode commencing "Avaunt, avaunt, 'tis holy ground," was written by Thomas Gray, the poet, the Regius Professor of Modern History, and set to music by Dr Randall, the Professor of Music. The ode, at the commencement following the installation of the Prince Consort in 1847, was written by William Wordsworth, the Poet Laureate, and set to music by Professor Walmisley. It may be added that when, during the Vice-Chancellorship of Dr John Peile, Master of Christ's, in the year 1892, Spencer Compton Cavendish Duke of Devonshire, succeeded his father

The Senate House

as shown on the medals struck at the installation
of the Duke of Northumberland as Chancellor
in 1840

as Chancellor, the witty Professor of Music (Sir) Charles Villiers Stanford caused applause and laughter among the undergraduates by introducing into his setting of the ode, the repeated refrain of the well-known hunting song, "D'ye ken John Peel?"

An installation medal was generally struck in connection with the ceremonies at the first visit of a new Chancellor—on the obverse there appears a portrait, and on the reverse a picture of the interior of the Senate House. At the installation of the Duke of Northumberland, in the year 1840, two medals were struck, the reverse of one representing the exterior of the Senate House, with an academic procession.

THE VICE-CHANCELLOR

ACCORDING to the new Statutes (D. Chap. III)
the Vice-Chancellor is to be elected annually by the
Regent House. "At the election of a Vice-Chancellor,
the Proctors shall stand in scrutiny with the two senior
members of the Regent House present. The scrutineers
shall first give their own votes in writing and then take
the votes in writing of all persons present who have the
right of voting. That one of the two persons nominated, for whom the greater number of votes is given,
shall be declared to be elected."

Looking back, we find that the Chancellor was
required generally to be in residence, but that, if he
were absent for more than fifteen days, a Vice-Chancellor (*vicarius*) was appointed. Dr Tanner, in *The
Historical Register*, gives a list of such offices from early
in the fifteenth century; two centuries later, when Dr
Fisher was chosen as Chancellor for life, the Vice-
Chancellor's standing increased in importance; and
when the Chancellor was a non-resident magnate,
his substitute became the leading official at Cambridge.

It is not necessary here to record all the details of the

Phot. Palmer Clarke

The Essex Cup

election of the Vice-Chancellor; but certain of the proceedings at his installation may be noticed.

First of all, it may be pointed out that formerly a collection of books descended from generation to generation through the hands of successive Vice-Chancellors. A list of these may be seen in MS. CVI, C.C.C., signed "bie mee Walter Haddon," Master of Trinity Hall, and passed on to his successor Dr Madew in 1550. Again, as pointed out in *The Cambridge Portfolio* (p. 157), there existed at St Catharine's College "a catalogue of ye Vice-Chancellor's bookes delivered to me Thomas Browne by Dr Stanley, and by me to Dr Eachard" 1695. There were more than twenty books and MSS. Some of them are still at the Registry, including Hare's *Collections*.

John Beverley, in his *Account of the Different Ceremonies observed in the Senate House* (1788), pp. 19, 20, says, in describing the resignation of the Vice-Chancellor's office, "the Proctors, preceded by the Bedells, come to the Vice-Chancellor's Place, at the West End of the Senate House; where a Bench is placed for them to sit on. After a little Stay, they go to the Table; and the late Vice-Chancellor delivers to them, the Statute Book; the Seals; Keys; Purse and Plate." These, "together with the other books" mentioned above, were handed to the new Vice-Chancellor on his admission.

But the full *Order of Proceedings* is given at the end of this section.

Sir Arthur Shipley, in a beautifully illustrated article in *Country Life*, 6 December, 1919, describes some of these *Insignia* or *Regalia*; adding the Maces, and including among the Plate, the Cup and the Rings.

The University Seal is kept at the Registry in an elaborate case, which has three keys, one retained by the Vice-Chancellor, and two declared to be kept by the Proctors; but now in the possession of the Registrary. The Plate includes the beautiful Cup presented, in 1592-3, by the second Earl of Essex, and inscribed with the Devereux arms, and the Gold Signet Rings—a large thumb-ring with the University arms, and a smaller ring representing Minerva with her helmet, shield and spear, with a motto, "Si perdam, pereo." Of this Sir Arthur Shipley (by whose permission they are here figured) gives a humorous translation. On the inner surface is the motto in English, "My only rest."

The Maces will be described when we treat of the *Esquire Bedells*.

The Vice-Chancellor's Rings

ORDER OF PROCEEDINGS ON OCTOBER I

RESIGNATION AND ADMISSION OF VICE-CHANCELLOR

9.30 a.m.

The Vice-Chancellor ſtands behind the Chair—the Esquire Bedell calls "Magiſtri."

The Vice-Chancellor then makes his speech.

The Proctors sit together on the Throne, and then come to the table in the Vice-Chancellor's place.

The Vice-Chancellor hands to the Proctors his rings, keys, cup, etc., the Senior Proctor taking charge of the purse.

The Ex-Vice-Chancellor then withdraws.

The new Vice-Chancellor robes at the entrance to the Senate House, and is brought to the dais by a Bedell without a ſtaff. He then takes his seat on one of the chairs and puts on his cap.

He next takes off his cap and comes to the south side of the table; the Proctors occupying the Vice-Chancellor's usual place.

The Senior Proctor reads the affirmation, to which the Vice-Chancellor replies "Ita do fidem." The Senior Proctor then takes the Vice-Chancellor's right hand and admits him to office in the usual form of words.

The Vice-Chancellor goes to his place at the table, and the Proctors, standing at the sides, hand to the Vice-Chancellor the rings, keys, purse, and cup.

The Proctors then take their leave and go to their table.

The Vice-Chancellor takes his seat on the Throne.

If the Vice-Chancellor wishes to make a speech he goes to the back of the Chair, the Bedell calling "Magistri."

The Vice-Chancellor sits on the Chair and dissolves the Congregation.

He then takes off his cope.

See the conclusion of the election of the Proctors on the same morning.

THE REGISTRARY

THE REGISTRARY is one of the moſt important
adminiſtrative University officers: he has to deal with
records and documents, with congregations and
councils and courts, with Boards and Syndicates, with
the *Reporter*, and to some extent with fees and moneys
(though that rising official the Treasurer may perhaps
in the future supersede him in some of these laſt
matters). But in the Senate House he does not thruſt
himself forward, and so in dealing with Ceremonies
we have not much to say about the Regiſtrary.

But his office is fairly ancient, appearing, and de-
finitely appearing, at the beginning of the sixteenth
century. The firſt Regiſtrary was Robert Hobbs, who,
like all those who held the poſt in that century, was
an Esquire Bedell and an expert in all University
affairs. Even after he resigned office in the year 1543,
there is a curious record of how the old gentleman was
consulted as to the correct way of carrying out academic proceedings. His successor John Mere left three
or four Diaries which throw much light upon University ceremonies; and Matthew Stokes, who followed
him, was one of the keeneſt of all the Cambridge

officials. He gave "a curious picture of all the habits of the several degrees and officers of the University," which formerly hung in the Consistory, but is now somewhat inconveniently placed on the staircase of the Registry.

Fuller says of him (*Worthies of Buckinghamshire*):

a Register he was indeed both by his place and painful performance therein: for he (as the Poets fain of Janus with two faces) saw two worlds that before and after the Reformation. In such junctures of time, so great the confusion and embezzling of records, that had not Master Stokes been the more careful, I believe that though Cambridge would not be so oblivious as Messala Corvinus who forgot his own name, yet would she have forgotten the names of all her ancient officers. To secure whose succession to posterity, Mr Stokes with great industry and fidelity collected a Catalogue of Chancellors, Vice Chancellors and Proctors. He was a zealous Papist (even unto the persecution of others), which I note, not to disgrace his memory, but defend myself, for placing him before the Reformation, though he lived many years in the reign of Queen Elizabeth.

There were four Registraries in the sixteenth century; but only three of these officers spanned the seventeenth. The first of them, James Tabor of Corpus, lived on till the time of the Civil War, and left a *Book* dealing with Ceremonies and University customs; and so did his successor, who survived almost till the Revolution.

The eighteenth century saw six Registraries, of whom Lynford Caryl (afterwards Master of Jesus College) left many writings in the Registry including an important Index of Documents, etc.; while his successor Henry Hubbard, of Emmanuel, also bequeathed a *Book* of curious records.

During the nineteenth century, there was a remarkable succession of keen and able Registraries, including William Huſtler, Joseph Romilly, Henry Richards Luard and John Willis Clark—whose care and skill among our academic documents and records are the admiration of all who may consult the archives of the University.

Dr Keynes, who worthily maintained the reputation of the office for sixteen years (1910-25), has been succeeded by Mr E. Harrison, of Trinity.

THE PROCTORS

THESE OFFICERS have long played a leading part in the administration of University affairs. Of old, indeed, they had yet more prominent duties. Dr Tanner thus sums up their miscellaneous functions: "In earlier times it was their duty to regulate the hours of disputing and lecturing, of burial services, inceptions, and festivals, and to act for the University in all kinds of business. They destroyed bad herrings exposed for sale, bought vestments, bell-ropes, and candlesticks, and had charge of the University Chest. They also patrolled the streets to repress disturbances, and exercised jurisdiction over improper persons." They still have the right to enter licensed premises and places of public entertainment. They have the power of fining undergraduates for the infringing of certain regulations; and the Duke of York a while back laughingly referred to "the six-and-eightpence" of which he was mulcted when *in statu pupillari*.

Dr Duckworth (Fellow of Jesus College, who was Senior Proctor in the years 1904-5), after he had resigned office, published (*C.A.S. Proceedings*, XLVII. 448-54) some interesting Notes on *The Proctor's Hal-*

Phot. Stearn

A Junior Proctor with his "bull-dogs"

berd and other Insignia, quoting learned observations by Lord Dillon. At his installation at the beginning of the academic year, the Senior Proctor comes into possession of a Linstock and a Partisan, and the Junior Proctor receives at the same time a Halberd and a Butter measure. The Senior Proctor's "staff" was presented to the University by John Townsend, Esq., of Norfolk, in the year 1591. The illustration here reproduced shows the Junior Proctor of 1902 with his "men," popularly known as "bull-dogs," one of them holding the Halberd, the other the Butter measure and one of the *books* carried on important official occasions. These are sometimes alluded to as "Bibles"; but they really are editions of *Statuta Academiae Cantabrigiensis,* printed by J. Archdeacon in 1785; the 600 printed pages are followed by many manuscript additions in the writing of subsequent Registraries—Messrs Borlase, Pemberton, Hustler, Romilly—down to the year 1855.

The so-called Butter measure was described (with a figure) by Mr W. B. Redfern (*C.A.S. Proceedings,* XLVI, 221, 222). It is now preserved in the Registry.

With regard to the dress of the Proctors, it may be noted that, when attending special ceremonies in the Senate House, they wear what is called "the Congregation Habit," viz. a hood worn in the ordinary way—

over *the ruff*, which is itself worn over the gown; but when attending the University Church, they wear "the Ad Clerum Habit," which is a squared hood, with three buttons in front, without the ruff. The Senior Proctor wears a bow on the right shoulder over the ruff; the Junior Proctor wears one on the left shoulder.

The nomination of the Proctors is vested in the Colleges. In every year two Colleges nominate persons for Proctors in the order prescribed in a fifty years' cycle. If a vacancy occurs during the year, Trinity Hall (which was not included in the order established in the year 1514) nominates and presents a person for election.

Pro-Proctors are also appointed; and lately a Pro-Proctor has been added in connection with the regulation of motor-cars and motor-cycles.

Here is given the order of proceedings in connection with the resignation and election of Proctors.

RESIGNATION AND ELECTION OF PROCTORS

10 a.m. [On 1 October, following the Admission of the Vice-Chancellor.]

The Proctors give up their books, etc., to the Vice-Chancellor at the table and retire. The Esquire Bedell reads the Statute (Paragraphs 3 and 4 on page 16, Edition 1914), also a paper supplied by the Registrary "Nominati et praesentati, etc." The two senior Masters of Arts present then take the Proctors' usual position and read Graces for the appointment of the Proctors, as prepared by the Registrary.

The Proctors elect go to the lower end of the Senate House and put on Congregation habit; they then advance to the Vice-Chancellor at the table.

The Vice-Chancellor reads the affirmation and form of admission to each in turn, taking each by the right hand when admitting him.

The Vice-Chancellor hands them their books, etc.

The Pro-Proctors are admitted if present.

The Vice-Chancellor then takes the Chair and dissolves the Congregation.

The Vice-Chancellor, preceded by the Esquire Bedells, proceeds to his Lodge, and outside the door of the Lodge receives the congratulations of such Members of the Senate as follow him from the Senate House. This would naturally follow immediately after the Congregation at which he was admitted, but, as the next Congregation begins at 10 a.m., there is not sufficient time.

Note. After the admission of the Pro-Proctors, and before the dissolving of the Congregation, ordinary Graces (if any) may be read.

At about 11.15 a.m., the Vice-Chancellor generally again attends the Senate House, for the swearing in of the University Constables.

THE ESQUIRE BEDELLS

PERHAPS the moſt picturesque officers connected with the University are the *Bedells*. They reach back to the earlieſt times; though their former somewhat homely attendances have developed into the dignified duties of the Esquire Bedells, and their primitive wooden ſtaves into elaborate silver Maces. They are thus linked with our oldeſt functions; and they are concerned with our lateſt ceremonies.

They were almoſt always men of subſtance, at leaſt as compared with our poor scholars; they generally held some other occupation; and the early liſts of benefactors contain a remarkable number of Univer- sity Beadles. Later on from being merely "privileged persons," they became Esquire Bedells, and the office has long been held by diſtinguished graduates.

In the latter part of the fifteenth century, the three Bedells—for there were formerly three of these officers— were classed as the Bedell of Divinity (and Canon Law), the Bedell of Arts, and the "other Bedell." It may at once be ſtated that in the middle of the nineteenth century, on the death of Mr Leapingwell, of Corpus, the third Bedellship was abolished; but, before this, they had long been accounted "equal," though the oldest in office was always called "the Senior Bedell."

As they generally served for many years, and, as the technicalities of the many ceremonies were often intricate, they naturally became the storehouse of information and precedent. We have seen how, in the year when Nicholas Ridley was Proctor (1533-4), old Mr Hobbs, though he had retired from office, was consulted on some disputed question; and the following record may be quoted from a document in the Registry: Caryl, xv. 103 (4): "*Query.* At what time does the University year end? *Answered* by Bedles Hughes and J. Buck; that it ends on the Friday in Commencement week."

But not only have there been verbal answers and traditional reports; many of the Bedells have committed to writing and then to print their remembrances of old customs and ceremonies. We have already alluded to the records of the first four Registraries and remarked that they were all also Esquire Bedells. We may add that Dean Peacock, at the end of his learned and judicious *Observations* on the Statutes of our University, has printed long and exceedingly interesting extracts from two old books (copied by Wm Cole the antiquary) by Matthew Stokes and John Buck—

An Esquire Bedell (1815) with a Yeoman Bedell

the former including notices from pre-Reformation records, and the latter dealing with Restoration customs.

Later on John Beverley (Esquire Bedell from 1770
to 1827) published in the year 1788 an *Account of the
different Ceremonies* observed in the Senate House; ten
years later Adam Wall issued a similar work, which
was re-edited in 1828 by Henry Gunning (Esquire
Bedell from 1789 to 1854). These three compilers were
all members of Christ's College.

It is impossible to refer to the Esquire Bedells without emphasising the elaborate *Maces* which they carry
before the Chancellor or the Vice-Chancellor on all
official occasions. There is in the *Proceedings* of the
Cambridge Antiquarian Society for the year 1879
(pp. 207-19) a very accurate and interesting account,
by the late Mr A. P. Humphry, of the Maces, one of
which was borne by him, with great dignity, for many
years (1877 to 1913). They are illustrated with careful
drawings; and fine photographs of these appear in Sir
Arthur Shipley's article mentioned above. They are
here reproduced by permission.

The Maces were presented by George Villiers, Duke
of Buckingham, Chancellor in 1626. They are en-
graved with the Royal Arms, and the arms, crest, and
badge of the donor, and each (we are speaking of the
three Maces formerly used) has three mottoes taken

from Latin editions of the Bible, or from classical
authors. (One has a curious misspelling.) "Each mace
consists of five hollow pieces, which are built upon a
wooden stick, and held fast to it by silver screws."

In the pictures of the Coats of Arms at the heads
of the Maces as given by the Master of Christ's in his
article in *Cambridge Cameos*, it will be noticed that
the arms and edging of those now in use are almost
obliterated owing to the habit of carrying the maces
reversed and grounding them when the Esquire Bedells
come to a standstill.

Before the Sovereign and before the Chancellor, the
maces are carried upright, not slanting and resting on
the shoulder of the Bedell. When the Sovereign visits
the University, the Staves are surrendered; though they
are usually almost immediately restored to, and re-
sumed by the Esquire Bedells.

When the third Bedellship was abolished in the year
1863, the corresponding Mace was deposited in the
Registry; but it is now in the keeping of the Vice-
Chancellor.

Formerly there was another Mace carried by an in-
ferior officer known as the Yeoman Bedell, or the Dog
Bedell, who formed a somewhat picturesque figure
in processions, in proclamations, etc., and who performed certain duties in connection with the courts,

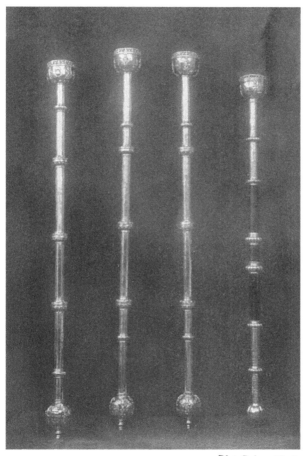

Phot. Palmer Clarke

The Maces

the markets and so on. This office was abolished in the year 1858; and the Mace rested in the Registry during the remainder of the nineteenth century; but at the installation of Lord Rayleigh in 1908 the Mace of the Yeoman Bedell was borne by the University Marshal, and it is now usually carried in processions.

It will be pointed out in the section on *Obsolete Officers* that, in early days, the official who was known as the Master of Glomery was entitled to be preceded by a Bedell.

The dress of the Esquire Bedell was formerly, on important occasions, imposing. At the installation as Chancellor of the Duke of Monmouth in 1674, we are told that "the Junior Bedle Mr William Worts went first in his Bedle's Gown Velvet Cap Gold Hat-band and Regent's Hood, holding the Bedle's Staff the round End upward.... The two other Esquire Bedles were habited as the former."

When a deputation in 1753 waited on the then Chancellor (the Duke of Newcastle) at Newmarket, we learn, from the *Journal* of the Registrary Mr Hub-bard, the Bedells wore tufted gowns, hoods, coifs and round caps.

It has long been customary for a new Chancellor to present to the Senior Esquire Bedell a gold neck chain and badge, the latter bearing the arms of the

University worked in enamel "as a memorial of his election as Chancellor." During the long services of John Beverley (1770-1827), of Henry Gunning* (1789-1854), of Alfred Paget Humphry (1877-1913), these officers were on two or three occasions each the recipient of a chain, and Mr A. H. Evans was similarly decorated before his retirement in 1920.

Under the headings of *Processions* and *Degrees*, we shall have occasion to refer in detail to the duties and ceremonies connected with the office of these distinguished University officials.

* In the well-known picture of this Esquire Bedell in the Combination Room at Christ's College, he is represented as wearing a "badge" only.

MATRICULATION

No one (it is ſtated in the New Statutes) shall be matriculated unless he is presented by a College, or has been approved as a Non-Collegiate Student; and is qualified in certain ways, such as, by having been approved as a Research Student, or as an Affiliated Student, etc. etc. (see Statute B).

The University may determine by Ordinance the manner of matriculation (see B. 1. 2).

Dr Venn, in the Introdu&ion to his volume, the *Book of Matriculations and Degrees,* has an intereſting se&ion on the old Matriculation Regiſter. He says that by the Statute of 1544 every ſtudent was required to matriculate soon after commencing residence, but the names of many ſtudents who certainly entered at a College and came into a&ual residence are not recorded. Sometimes the omission was due to the youth of the ſtudent. Again fellow-commoners, and other young men of family, who seldom contemplated taking a degree, often negle&ed to present themselves to the Regiſtrary—Oliver Cromwell is a signal inſtance in point; but in the case of those who graduated, there are not a few cases where no matriculation is on record.

In other cases, matriculation was delayed till juſt before graduation. Lord Byron, for inſtance (probably
from financial reasons), did not matriculate till the
same day (4 July 1808) on which he was presented for
his M.A. degree.

CONGREGATIONS AND GRACES

THE University has power to prescribe from time to time by Grace the form and manner of holding a Con- gregation, the conditions under which Graces, having received the sanction of the Council, may be offered to the Senate, the mode of taking votes and recording results, and generally to regulate its own proceedings.

Graces which are offered to the Senate for its sanction are read at a Congregation by the Senior Proctor. Any member of the Senate who objects to any Grace may signify his opposition by pronouncing the words "Non placet" immediately after such Grace has been read. The Senior Esquire Bedell calls "Ad Scruti- nium," and other members of the Senate desiring to vote then take their places, sitting down, on the Placet (south) and Non placet (north) sides respectively of the Senate House. If in the opinion of both the Proctors the result of the division is obvious, the Senior Proctor declares the result forthwith, without taking the votes singly; but any two members of the Senate may request the Vice-Chancellor to direct that the votes be taken singly. In this event the vote is taken on cards provided for the purpose, the count being made, and the result announced, by the Proctors.

SUPPLICATS

THE theory in conferring degrees is that the candidate applies to the University for the degree to be conferred in a formal petition, called a *Supplicat,* which is presented on his behalf by the Praelector of his College. These Supplicats are read to the Senate by the Senior Proctor, and after the reading of each Grace he says "Placet," raising his cap; which means that the Senate passes a Grace for the conferring of the degree. The practice is that after each group (for D.D., M.A., B.A., etc.) the Senior Proctor says "Omnes placent."

There are special forms of Supplicat for each kind of degree. These are printed in the *Ordinances.*

DEGREES

W E may at once describe the Procedure on the days of General Admission to Degrees—at the end of the Easter Term, in the month of June—after the issue of the Tripos Lists.

It may be noted that the names of the three classes of the successful candidates in the Mathematical Tripos— the Wranglers, the Senior Optimes and the Junior Optimes—in alphabetical order—are still proclaimed by the Moderators and Examiners in the Senate House; printed copies being thrown among the waiting under⁄ graduates and students of Girton and Newnham. The same proceeding holds with regard to certain other Triposes.

On the Saturday, the first day for General Admis⁄ sion for Ordinary Degrees, at a Congregation at 9.30 a.m. the Supplicats are presented to the Senate for approval—the fees having been paid previously, and the Book of Subscriptions being signed in the Senate House.

A second Congregation is held at 11 a.m., the B.A.'s being admitted from the Colleges in turn im⁄ mediately after presentation; the LL.B.'s follow, and those taking other degrees.

On the following Tuesday, there is again at 9.30 a.m. a presentation of Supplicats to the Senate for approval.

There are two other Congregations on the same day for the admission of those who have obtained Honours, etc. At the second Congregation at 11 a.m. after the presentation and admission of candidates for higher degrees than B.A., LL.B., or Mus.B., candidates for the degree of B.A. are presented and admitted from Colleges in the following order: King's, Trinity, St John's, Peterhouse, Clare, Pembroke, Gonville and Caius, and Trinity Hall in alphabetical order in each College; any LL.B.'s and Mus.B.'s are presented and admitted afterwards. A third Congregation is held at 2 p.m. when similar proceedings take place as to the candidates from Corpus Christi and the other colleges, from Selwyn College Public Hostel and from the Non-Collegiate Students (Fitzwilliam House). The candidates are required to wear proper academic dress over dark clothing.

In each case the Praelectors present their Students (or the Fathers present their Sons, as the expression used to read), four at a time giving their right hands to the Praelector, each Student taking hold of a finger. The candidate kneels and places his hands together for the Vice-Chancellor to admit him.

Admission of the Senior Wrangler in 1842

King's College comes first as a special Royal Foundation; Trinity and St John's* also have royal privileges; the other Colleges following the order of their foundation; Selwyn and the Non-Collegiate Students completing the order.

Doctors wear scarlet.

[In the Admission to Degrees, the names of some are asterisked in the printed list: these are those who are admitted *in absentia*. The Praelectors represent them by proxy.]

THE SENIOR WRANGLER, AND THE WOODEN SPOON

It will be noticed that in the above account of the Procedure at Admission to Degrees the expression "in alphabetical order" occurs more than once. Formerly, however, the "order of merit" as a result of the various examinations was very prominent; and in particular—in the Mathematical Tripos—the Senior Wrangler at the head of the list, and "the Wooden Spoon" bringing up the rear, added great zest to the proceedings. The honour accorded to the former, and the ironical cheers which greeted the latter, were a distinguishing

* Why has not Christ's, the other College connected with the Lady Margaret Beaufort, claimed the same privileges?

feature of the proceedings. But when, in the year 1911, the names appeared for the firſt time in alphabetical order, these curious and charaſteriſtic old Cambridge cuſtoms became obsolete.

THE TRIPOS

Here, if we were writing a hiſtory or giving an anti⹀ quarian record, we might go further back, and give an account of the old disputations, the responsions and opponencies, and so on.* It will suffice to quote from the quaint description of the ancient Determinations on Ash Wednesday—as given in the Appendix A of Dean Peacock's *Observations*, p. x:

When every man is placed, the Senior Proſtor shall, with some oration, shortly move the Father to begyn, who after his Exhortation unto his Children, shall call fourthe his eldeſt sone,† animate hym

* A glance backward may be made at the old process known as "huddling." If a candidate for a degree had not performed all the required exercises, he was required, before his Supplicat was presented to the Caput to go into the Sophs' School and *huddle* for those he had not kept. Whereupon some trifling and ludicrous proceedings fol⹀ lowed. The name is said to be derived from the fact that "when Queſtiones, etc. came down from the Gallery of the Senate House, at a given signal '*hoodling*' began, *i.e.* each man's bedmaker put his rabbit's fur hood over his head."

† He is called the *bachelor of the ſtool*, or *tripos*, which gave the name to the day: he was generally seleſted for his skill and readiness in dis⹀ putation, and was allowed, like the *prævaricator* at the *majora comitia,* and the *terræ filius* at Oxford, considerable license of language, a privilege which was not unfrequently abused.

Presentation of the Wooden Spoon

to dispute with an old Bachilour, which shall sit upon a ſtoole before Mr. Proctours, unto whome the sone shall propounde 2 Queſtions, & in bothe them shall the sone dispute, etc.

In the very curious account of Queen Mary's visitation in 1556 (see Dr Lamb's *Original Documents, C.C.C.C.*) we find the following notice of the proceedings on Ash Wednesday:

On Asshewendesday, rayne and snow together. It. Mʳ Bronſted & I [John Mere] had in all the Bachelors before viii (at St Maryes), & shortly after the Vicechancellor began his sermon in S. Maryes, thuniversite Bell (*the school Bell*), & allso St Maryes Bell rynginge to the same, the Mayre and Aldermen being presente. It. the acte began before x & continued tyll halfe howre after iii no senioryte given, no byll made nor none called, but only ii of the seniors the Vic. and D. Sedgewycke were present from the begininge to the latter ende, Mʳ Turner, Father, Syr Whytgyfte the bachelor (*of the ſtool*), Syr Brydges the eldeſt son, Mʳˢ Otway, and Malyn replyed upon the bachelors & onlye Mʳ Hutton apon the Father.

It may be added that Syr Whytgyfte was afterwards Archbishop of Canterbury, and Mr Hutton, Archbishop of York. The title of Syr was given to all bachelors, whether of arts, law, or physic.

Returning to the present conferring of degrees, it may be remarked that candidates for the Degrees of D.D. or B.D., LL.D., M.D., and Mus.D. are presented by the Regius Professors of Divinity, Law, and Physic, and the Professor of Music, respectively, or by their deputies. Candidates for other Doctors' Degrees,

S   3

etc., are presented by the Chairman of their Special Board of Studies or by Doctors of their faculties (or their deputies), who wear copes for the occasion.

"Bachelors in Arts, Law," etc. (the quotation is from the section on Admission to Degrees in the *University Calendar*) remain "'Bachelors designate' until the 31st of December... following their admission to the Degree; on this day they become full Bachelors by a procedure of 'Inauguration,' at which they are not required to be present. Similarly Masters and Doctors only attain the full Degree by 'Creation,'... on the 30th of June.... Candidates for the Master's Degree are known as 'Inceptors' between the date of their admission to the Degree and the date of their 'Creation.'" But the New Statutes have altered this.

When a Jew or other non-Christian is admitted to a degree, the Vice-Chancellor, instead of referring to the Holy Trinity, may use the expression "In nomine Dei," but he must be informed beforehand of the presentation. Some time since a Jew, bearing a characteristic name, stated to his Praelector his wish to have the simple expression used. At the presentation that official had forgotten to inform the Vice-Chancellor and was about to introduce the student, when the latter protested and asked on principle for a separate presentation. The Father, anxious that the pro-

The last Wooden Spoon

ceedings should not be interrupted, was equal to the occasion and noticed that the candidate was wearing brown shoes. This is contrary to the regulations, and the Praelector said that the presentation must be postponed. Whereupon the student at once withdrew his objections and was presented with the others taking their degrees—his principles being hidden and his brown shoes ignored.

It may be added that, at another University recently, a Jew was to be admitted and due notice had been given; but the Vice-Chancellor had forgotten the right formula, and to cover his confusion pronounced, with much unction, the expression, "In nomine Dei OMNIPOTENS." It was magnificent but it was not grammar!

COMMENCEMENT DAY

THE ceremonies of the "creation" of Masters and Doctors on Commencement Day, by which the degree was "made perfect," is now a mere signing of lists, or a reading of names (as Dr Tanner remarks, *Historical Register*, p. 186), but it was formerly a proceeding of considerable solemnity. Gunning, in his *Reminiscences* (1, 26), describes a Commencement Sunday at Cambridge:

> The College walks were crowded. Every doctor in the University wore his scarlet robes during the whole day. All the noblemen appeared in their splendid robes, not only at St Mary's and in the College Halls, but also in the public walks. Their robes (which are now [1785] uniformly purple) at that time were of various colours, according to the tastes of the wearers—purple, white, green, and rose-colour, were to be seen at the same time. The people from the neighbouring villages then never ventured to pass the rails which separate the walks from the high road. The evening of *Commencement* Tuesday, if not the most numerous, was always the most splendid assemblage at *Pot Fair*, when the merits of the steward and the events of the *Ball* formed the chief subjects of conversation.

The steward just mentioned was chosen by the ladies from among the noblemen, who generally took their degree on the Monday. (See Wordsworth's *University Society in the Eighteenth Century*, p. 276.) In the same volume may be seen specimens of the *Music Speeches*, and the *Odes* set to music on such occasions.

At a later date, we read in the *Memoirs of the late J. W. Clark*, by Sir A. E. Shipley, p. 44, a description by the late Registrary of the social importance of *Commencement*.

On Commencement Sunday the whole academic world used to walk up and down [on Clare Hall Piece, the green space in front immediately to the west of the College,] for half an hour after the University Sermon, and a very pretty sight it was, Mr Vice-Chancellor and all the Heads and Doctors in scarlet, and the ladies in their best frocks. In [those] days... personal attendance was required at "creation."... It was a time of festivity in a quiet way, and much looked forward to as the last occasion when all the men of a given year had the chance of meeting each other.

INSIGNIA DOCTORALIA

THE *insignia doctoralia* formerly used at the creation of University Doctors consisted of a Cap and a Kiss, a Book and a Ring, and a Chair. These are described and their significance explained in an elegant oration delivered by Dr Bentley in his speech (prefixed to his edition of Terence) upon the creation of Dr Mawson and six others at the Commencement in 1725. This is reprinted by Dean Peacock in his *Observations* (Appendix A, p. xl, etc.) and by Sir John Sandys, in his article on Ancient University Ceremonies in the volume issued in honour of Mr J. W. Clark, in 1909. Sir Arthur Shipley has described it in *Country Life* (6 December 1919), where he humorously re-marks that "the kiss was mercifully done away with long before my time, and, perhaps, in view of the increasing demand of ladies for degrees, it is just as well. Still it is but just to state that Bentley records it was 'no kiss of dalliance (*suavium*) but a kiss of holy love (*osculum*).'"

Sir John Sandys records a personal incident of much interest. He says:

1858. More than fifty years ago, being then a boy of fourteen, during a visit to an elder brother at Corpus, I was admitted to the galleries of the Senate-House, and there had the satisfaction of seeing the 'gold ring' actually used at the conferring of a doctor's degree. The Senior Esquire Bedell on that occasion was Mr George Leapingwell, of Corpus, who held office from 1826 to 1863; and I remember distinctly that the recipient of the degree seemed rather reluctant to part with the ring, and that the Bedell had to prompt him persistently to return it. I have repeatedly mentioned this incident to members of the University far older than myself, but they have no recollection of having ever seen such a ceremony. I have therefore thought it right to put this fact on record as almost certainly the very latest occasion on which the sole surviving portion of this ancient ceremony was observed in Cam-bridge.

If the antiquary [says the late Dean Rashdall, *Universities,* 1895, II, 643] wants to see a true mediaeval *cappa,* he must go to Cambridge on a degree day. There he will find the presiding Vice-Chancellor and the Professors who present for degrees in the Superior Faculties arrayed in a garment which exactly resembles a fourteenth century miniature of the Chancellor con-tained in the precious *Chancellors' Book* of Oxford. It is a sleeveless scarlet cloak lined with miniver with a tippet and hood of the same material fastened thereto.

HONORARY DEGREES

THE following is a copy of the regulations issued at a recent conferring of Degrees; the Chancellor being present:

TUESDAY, 9 JUNE 1925

The Recipients of Honorary Degrees are requested to assemble in the Arcade of the University Library not later than 11.50 a.m. They will there sign their names in the Registrary's Book. After the book has been signed by all, the Chancellor's procession will form.

The recipients of Honorary Degrees will join the procession in the following order:

(1) VISCOUNT CAVE	(2) MR J. H. WHITLEY
(3) THE EARL OF READING	(4) LORD BEARSTEAD
(5) LORD BRADBURY	(6) SIR F. POLLOCK
(7) SIR H. J. NEWBOLT	(8) PROFESSOR JOLY
(9) MR A. P. MAUDSLEY	(10) SIR H. P. ALLEN

Seats for the Recipients of Honorary Degrees will be reserved in the first instance below the dais of the Senate House.

The Recipients will be presented to the Chancellor by the Public Orator in the above-mentioned order.

Each Recipient in turn will be conducted by one of the Esquire Bedells to a point below the dais in front of the Chancellor, marked on the accompanying plan with an asterisk. The Public Orator will stand on the right of the Chancellor.

At the end of his speech the Public Orator will announce the name of the Recipient and, taking him by the right hand, will conduct him to the Chancellor. The Chancellor will rise, and taking the Recipient by the right hand, will admit him to the Degree. The Recipient will then be conducted by one of the Esquire Bedells to his seat on the dais among the Doctors.

Here it may be noted the recipient of an Honorary Degree on being presented stands; the Chancellor or the Vice-Chancellor taking him by the right hand; but for an ordinary Degree, the recipient kneels, puts his hands together, and the Vice-Chancellor puts his hands outside the recipient's hands.

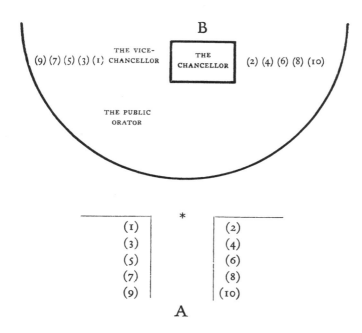

The accompanying plan indicates the seats assigned to the Recipients of Honorary Degrees. (A) below the dais, and (B) on the dais.
The numbers refer to the names in the above lift.

After the Congregation the Procession will leave the Senate House
in the order in which it entered. The Chancellor and the Recipients
of Honorary Degrees will then proceed to Downing College with
the Vice-Chancellor.

It is requefted that academical robes may be worn at the Vice-
Chancellor's luncheon.

UNIVERSITY COSTUME

ALREADY in almoſt every ſection of this work, some allusion has been made to the dress worn by some special officer or at some special funſtion or ceremony. We may here give a more detailed account of Uni- versity Coſtume. But it may firſt be remarked that there is a very excellent chapter on the subjeſt by Dr Tanner in *The Hiſtorical Regiſter*, which he so ably edited. The late Professor E. C. Clark wrote elaborate and learned treatises on "English Academical Cos- tume" and on "College Caps and Doſtors' Hats" (see *The Archaeological Journal*, L, 74, 137, 183, etc.). An article in the *Encyclopaedia Britannica* contains an intereſting illuſtrated ſection on Academic Coſtume. The piſture (1590) on the ſtaircase of the Regiſtry already referred to, and the remarkable drawings in Loggan's *Cantabrigia Illuſtrata* a century later will, of course, also be consulted.

In the old ſtatutes of our earlieſt College, Peterhouse, almoſt the opening words enjoin that a Fellow "will always appear in the University dressed in the proper robes (*veſtes*) of a scholar," while later on a special ſtatute (no. 35) is entitled *de Habitu Scolarium* and contains a reference to an ordinance issued by John de Stratford, Archbishop of Canterbury. Again, in the archives of Corpus Christi College there are re- ferences to the "liveries" (*liberatura*) worn by the Master, Fellows and Scholars; to benefactions made towards the same; and to their economical purchase at "Stirbitch Fair."

In the Peterhouse statute just quoted it is enacted that "the master and all and each of the scholars of our house shall adopt the clerical dress and tonsure, as becomes the condition of each," which reminds us that the question of academical dress was closely allied to that of clerical costume. Anthony Wood derives the dress from the *tunica talaris* and *cucullus* of the Bene- dictines.

It is not necessary here to quote University ordi- nances regulating academical dress (such as the Eliza- beth statutes of 1570, Lord Burghley's orders of 1587, the sumptuary commands of Charles II, and so on).

It may suffice briefly to refer to the chief articles of academical dress: the gown (*toga, roba,* or *tunica talaris*) so generally worn; the cope, worn over the gown, "probably originated in the ordinary *cappa clericalis,* or everyday mantle of the clergy. This kind of cope closed in front, and originally black in colour, is generally known as the *cappa clausa,* and sometimes, for con-

venience sake, had a slit in front to allow of the passage
of the hands. It was worn by Regent Masters when
lecturing and as a full dress by certain doctors. The
scarlet *cappa clausa* has survived to the present day at
Cambridge [as we have already noted] as the dress
worn by the Vice-Chancellor and by the Regius Professors of Divinity, Law, and Medicine, when pre-
senting for degrees."

The hood also was generally worn—though it
went out of fashion for undergraduates by the end of
the Tudor period. At Cambridge, as pointed out in
the *Encyclopaedia Britannica,* a distinction was made at
a later date between the hoods of non-Regents, which
were lined with silk, and those of Regents, which were
lined with miniver. Later again the Regents wore their
hoods in such a way as to show the white lining, while
the non-Regents arranged their hoods so that the white
did not show. Hence the name "White Hoods" and
"Black Hoods" given to the upper and lower houses
of the old Senate respectively. The *liri-pipe* was a
curious termination of the hood.

Till the 'thirties of the last century most students at
Cambridge wore a plain short black gown, as at Oxford; it was sleeveless, and was called "a curtain." In
the year 1828 it was agreed by the authorities at Corpus
"that the gown which has commonly been worn by

Undergraduates of this College be changed for one of the same gown as that commonly worn by Bachelors of Arts with the diſtinction of Velvet Facings." In 1836 the ſtudents of Clare received permission to change the form of their gowns, adopting a black gown with three broad velvet ſtripes on the sleeves, in imitaʼ tion of the *three chevrons gules* upon the College arms. Other Colleges followed with gowns with a disʼ tinction. But it ought to be pointed out that as Harʼ raden, in his *Coſtumes of the University of Cambridge*, published in 1805, ſtates: "The pensioners of Trinity College were already diſtinguished from all others by a Blue Gown with full sleeves made of Prince's ſtuff. The gowns of pensioners at Peterhouse, Queens', Trinity Hall, and King's are nearly the same as at Trinity except the former are all black."

Mr A. G. Almond, of Sidney Street, has published two intereſting booklets—one on *Cambridge Robes,* etc., the other entitled *Gowns and Gossip*; the former is beauʼ tifully illuſtrated; the latter contains authoritative inʼ formation as to the date of the variations of College gowns.

We have already (on p. 36) referred to the brave show made by the noblemen on Commencement Sunday; and further allusion might be made to the elaborate gowns worn by them and other fellowʼcommoners.

The queſtion of academic head-dress has been ela-
borately discussed in Professor E. C. Clark's *College
Caps and Doctors' Hats*, and in N. F. Robinson's
Pileus Quadratus. Formerly doctors wore a skull-cap
with an apex. Lord Burghley's letter in 1588 ordered
a round cap of velvet for doctors and a square cap of
cloth for graduates and scholars, with a round cloth
cap for other undergraduates. In the Middle Ages the
layman's head-dress was round, the parson's square.
Hence bonnets for all. The so-called Bishop Andrewes's Velvet Cap is generally worn by Doctors of
Divinity—other doctors wear a Bonnet, like a "beef-
eater's" cap. In the year 1769, Alexander Clere of
Corpus and others led a campaign againſt the *round*
cap worn by undergraduates, and the Chancellor, the
Duke of Grafton, consented that a change should be
made to a *square* one; "so all her scholars *square the
circle* now."

In a volume entitled *The Real Jew* (1925), an essay
by Rabbi Dr V. Schonfeld, it is claimed that the cap
and gown, though probably introduced by way of the
Church, are of Jewish origin. Complaints* were made
in the Middle Ages of Jews, who were wearing the

* See the celebrated inſtance in the *Epiſtolae Obscurorum Virorum*
("Magiſter Johannes Pelzer, to Magiſter Ortuin Gratius," vol. II).

black long coat and hat, that they were mistaken for priests or scholars, and, *horribile dictu*, were shown by passers-by the reverence due to those; and the Jews were forbidden to wear these clothes. The instructions as to the length of the garments to be worn by scholars are of Talmudic origin and codified by Maimonides. Round velvet caps of unquestionable Jewish origin (says Dr Schonfeld) are still worn on state occasions by Doctors in Law and Medicine in Oxford and Cambridge. Gascoigne, in his *Theological Dictionary*, naïvely declares that this ornament was bestowed by God Himself on the doctors of the Mosaic Law!

PROCESSIONS

W E have already had occasion several times to refer to the *Processions* which form so striking a feature in the Ceremonies of the University: but a separate section may be devoted to a subject involving so much etiquette. "You know your own degrees," says Mac-beth at the beginning of the Banquet Scene. Neverthe-less, the Registrary and the Esquire Bedells have much marshalling to do, or rather to arrange for, at various public functions.

In the New Statutes, the University *Administrative* Offices are given in the following order: "the offices of Chancellor, Vice-Chancellor, High Steward, Deputy High Steward, Commissary, Proctor, Orator, Registrary, Assistant Registrary, Librarian, Trea-surer, Director of the Fitzwilliam Museum, Esquire Bedell, Censor of Non-Collegiate Students."

The University *Teaching* Officers, according to the same New Statutes, are the Professors, Readers, Uni-versity Lecturers and University Demonstrators.

The following is the order of a Procession at a recent special conferring of Honorary Degrees (9 June 1925):

S   4

The Esquire Bedells.
THE CHANCELLOR
The University Marshal.
The Recipients of Honorary Degrees.
THE VICE-CHANCELLOR,
accompanied by the Registrary and the Orator.

The Proctors.
The Burgesses for the University.
Heads of Colleges.
The Regius Professor of Divinity.
The Regius Professor of Hebrew.
The Regius Professor of Greek,
Professors, if Doctors, in the order of their complete Degrees.

Doctors of Divinity.
Doctors of Law.
Doctors of Medicine.
Doctors of Science and of Letters.
Doctors of Music.
The Librarian.
The remaining Professors in the order of their appointment.

Members of the Council of the Senate.
Bachelors of Divinity.
Doctors of Philosophy.

The Procession is ordered to be formed under the Colonnade of the University Library. After the Congregation the Procession is to leave the Senate House in the order in which it entered, and to break off in Senate House Yard. There, to quote again from *Macbeth* (III. iv. 118), it may be said: "Stand not upon the order of your going."

It may be interesting to compare with this modern order of Procession, the following directions as given in Statute 174: *de generalibus processionibus.*

Ancient Order of Procession

1st   The Parochial Chaplains, walking, decently, with crucifixes and surplices, singing their Litany, till they come to a place to be appointed by the University.
2ndly the Friars of St Augustine;
3rdly the Friars of Mount Carmel;
4thly the Friars Minors;
5thly the Friars Preachers;
6thly the Brethren of the Hospital of St John the Evangelist;
7thly the Bachelors of the University;
8thly the Chaplains of the University;
9thly the Regent Masters;
10thly the Non-Regent Masters; and then the populace (*tunc plebs*).

Statute 175: *de habitibus in processionibus*, prescribes the habits to be worn in processions. Stokes's MS has some notes (see Peacock, Appendix A, pp. xvi and xvii) on the correct order followed by *opposing Canons, by opposing Monks, and by Inceptors* who were not gremials.

In Foxe's *Book of Martyrs* there is a curious picture of a sixteenth century Procession, reproduced in the

4-2

writer's *Esquire Bedells*, facing p. 37. This includes the Mayor and Corporation of Cambridge.

The Processions figured in the picture on the wall of the staircase in the Registry, before referred to (p. 12), should also be noticed.

THE PRESENTATION OF
AN ADDRESS TO H.M. THE KING

THE following is an example of the Procedure at the Presentation of an Address to His Majesty the King at one of the Royal Palaces, and the order of Procession on such an occasion.

On 14 March 1922 an address of congratulation on the marriage of Her Royal Highness Princess Mary was presented at Buckingham Palace to His Majesty the King, with whom was Her Majesty the Queen. The Address, approved by the Senate, was presented by the Chancellor, who was accompanied by the Vice-Chancellor, the two Representatives, the Senior and Junior Proctors, the Registrary, and six Members of the Senate nominated by the Vice-Chancellor. The Esquire Bedells with their maces preceded the Chancellor, who was attended by a train-bearer. "The Humble Address of the Chancellor, Masters, and Scholars of the University of Cambridge" was read by the Chancellor; and His Majesty the King graciously replied. The Chancellor then presented to their Majesties the Vice-Chancellor and one of the Masters.

THE BIDDING PRAYER

THE Bidding Prayer is not actually a prayer itself; it was anciently called "the Fourme of biddyng the Common Prayers." In the 1603 Canons, no. 55 is "the Form of a Prayer to be used (*imitanda*) by all Preachers before their Sermons (*in concionum ingressu*)." This Canon is founded upon the form in the Royal Injunctions of 1559, § liii, which was an expansion of the form in the Injunctions of 1547, § xxxvi, one still older being retained, with the omission of the Pope's name.

With regard to the specially added phrases used in the University—one of the few places where a Bidding Prayer is still recited—Dr Mullinger, in his *University History* (pp. 628-31), has an excellent Appendix (B) thereon. He even goes back to a sermon at Oxford on Ascension Day 1382 by a follower of Wyclif. He quotes the 1547 form referred to above, pointing out that the King is styled "Supreme Head."

In a sermon, by Bishop Jewell, preached at St Mary's, Oxford, and printed in his *Works* as issued by the Parker Society, a Bidding Prayer—with University applications—is given early in Edward the Sixth's reign.

The Bidding Prayer used by Dr Perne on the visit of Queen Elizabeth to Cambridge, in Auguſt 1564, is printed in Nichols' *Progresses*, III, 54.

Beverley, the Esquire Bedell, in his account of the University *Ceremonies* (1788), pp. 163, 164, gives the Latin form as used at that date. He adds after the Lord's Prayer, in reference to the following sermon, that the text should be given out firſt in Greek, then in Latin. As to the Chapter and Verse of the Text, he prints the form of announcement: "In Capite—— A.B. Commate—Sic se habet."

[Beverley adds that as a prayer before a Divinity Aĉt the colleĉt "Prevent us, O Lord, etc." should be used in Latin: *Aĉtiones noſtras singulas, Domine*, etc. (See the beginning of the Prayer at Sea and the end of the Ordination Service and of the Holy Communion).]

On one of the occasions when the present writer was Mayor's Chaplain at Cambridge, the then Bishop of Ely sanĉtioned a special form of the Bidding Prayer.

UNIVERSITY SERMONS

UNIVERSITY SERMONS are preached at Great St Mary's Church every Sunday during Full Term and on certain great Church Festivals such as Ascension Day, etc. Formerly special sermons were preached on a number of other occasions, such as the King's Accession, on the day of the Commemoration of Gunpowder Plot (November 5th), of the death of King Charles I (January 30th), etc. Still Commencement Sunday (the Sunday before the last Congregation in June) claims its special sermon; the Ramsden Sermon is preached on Whit Sunday; the Assize Sermon is also observed.

On Ash Wednesday the Litany is said; the Doctors of Divinity wearing copes. The Senior Proctor reads the Litany as far as the Lord's Prayer; the Vice-Chancellor finishes.

These sermons are preached at the University Church, as St Mary's the Great is frequently called, from its long association with academical functions. Back in the thirteenth century there are records of such a connection.

On Lady Day a University sermon is preached in the Chapel of King's College. It may be noted that on this occasion, by invitation of the Provost and Fellows, a select company of the University is entertained in the Provost's Lodge to chocolate and coffee and biscuits before the sermon; and the procession goes from the Lodge to the Chapel. After the sermon, the Provost conducts the Vice-Chancellor to the College gates. Such a sermon was also formerly delivered at St Botolph's, for we read in Mr Stokes's MS, that "on Saynt Vyncent Day in January there is a Dirige kepte att Saynt Botulphe Chyrche in Cambryge, att three of the clocke, to the whych commythe M Vice-chauncellar and the Proctars."

At St Benet's Church the Mere's Commemoration is still observed on Wednesday in Easter week; when various quaint customs are retained and payments are made. The sermon was instituted in 1559, in connection with John Mere an Esquire Bedell and University Registrary, who lived nearly opposite the church. The preacher receives 3s. 4d.; the Vice-Chancellor, 6d.; the proctors, the orator, and other officers have a groat each, the parish clerk 2d., and other gifts are made. There is a curious choice of subjects for the sermon.

THE ORATOR

In *The Historical Register of the University of Cambridge* is printed a list of the Public Orators since the beginning of the sixteenth century, commencing with the name of Richard Croke the Greek scholar. The duties of this officer are to be the mouthpiece and correspondent of the University. As footnotes to the list Dr Tanner has appended a most delightful store of personal anecdotes and illustrations. Such names are included as those of Sir Thomas Smith, Sir John Cheke, Roger Ascham, George Herbert, Christopher Wordsworth, Sir Richard Jebb and Sir John Sandys—the predecessor of the present Public Orator, Mr T. R. Glover.

Sir John Sandys, in the year 1910, published the *Orationes et Epistolae Cantabrigienses*, which he had spoken or written from the year 1876 when he was appointed after a memorable contest with that refined scholar Mr Charles Moule of Corpus. Till 1920 he continued to make elaborate speeches from the floor of the Senate House. Allusion has already been made (see p. 38) to an incident which occurred when, a schoolboy visiting his future University, he occupied a place in the gallery of that renowned building.

The Public Orator has from the firſt been entitled "to have precedence of all other Maſters of Arts; and, as a mark of honour, to walk in processions and sit in public aĉts separate from the reſt."

Gunning, at the beginning of the second volume of his *Reminiscences,* gives an extraordinary account of the goings⁄on in conneĉtion with a University Sermon, which used to be preached at Burwell, on Mid⁄Lent Sunday.

THE HIGH STEWARD

THE office of High Steward (*Senescallus Cancellarii*) has been occupied by men of the foremost position in the land—witness Sir Thomas More, Thomas Cromwell, Earl of Essex, Robert Cecil, Earl of Salisbury, Sir Edward Coke, Philip Yorke, Earl of Hardwicke (and his son of the same names and title), William Pitt, and other men of renown. His University Court is a court of record.

Nor should his deputy be forgotten.

"The provisions of the Statutes regarding the duration of tenure of the office of Chancellor and the manner of election to that office apply to the office of High Steward.

The Deputy High Steward shall be appointed by the High Steward by Letters Patent, but the appointment shall be subject to the approval of the Senate." (*Statutes*, D. IV.)

REPRESENTATION IN
PARLIAMENT

SINCE the beginning of the reign of James I, the University has been entitled to send two representatives to Parliament; and the honour has been keenly sought after. A long list of distinguished "burgesses" might be quoted. They are always conspicuous in University Processions.

The election of representatives of the University in Parliament now is governed by *The Representation of the People Act*, 1918 (8 Geo. V, chap. 64).

The University retains the right of sending two members to Parliament, which it has enjoyed since 1603, and this franchise may be exercised in addition to the ordinary franchise, but certain important changes have been made by the Act: (1) the right of voting is no longer restricted to Members of the Senate, but is extended to all graduates, and *includes women who would have been graduates if the University had granted Degrees to women students*; and (2) in order to promote the representation of minorities, each elector has only one *transferable vote*. The right of voting by proxy is still retained, in certain cases.

For the method of voting, see "The Proxy Paper (Universities) Order, 1918" (*Statutory Rules and Orders*, 1918, no. 1350), where the form of a proxy paper is set out and the regulations with regard to proxies are laid down.

THE COMMISSARY

THIS office has been held, since the sixteenth century, by a distinguished list of lawyers. The last holder, Mr J. F. P. Rawlinson, held office for more than a quarter of a century; during most of which time he was also one of the representatives of the University in Parliament.

"The Commissary shall be appointed by the Chancellor by Letters Patent." (*Statutes*, D. IV.)

UNIVERSITY DISCIPLINE;
THE *SEX VIRI*, ETC.

I N the New Statutes (B. VI) may be seen the section on *Discipline*, with its orders as to wearing of academical dress, the rendering obedience to persons in authority, its penalties and fines, etc. The disciplinary regulations are as follows. A court, called the ViceChancellor and the *Sex Viri*, the members of which shall be the ViceChancellor and six persons elected singly by Grace for two years, shall have jurisdiction over University officers and over such persons not *in statu pupillari* as hold degrees or titles of degrees. Five members of the court shall constitute a quorum.

As a court of appeal the ViceChancellor and the *Sex Viri* shall hear appeals from decisions of the General Board, or other body, depriving a University officer of his office on account of failure to perform satisfactorily the duties or to fulfil the conditions of tenure of his office, and shall affirm or reverse such decisions. The judgment of the ViceChancellor and the *Sex Viri* in such cases shall be final.

As a court of first instance the ViceChancellor and the *Sex Viri* shall adjudicate when persons over whom they have jurisdiction are charged otherwise than as aforesaid with offences against the discipline of the University or with grave misconduct. Every decision of the court acting as a court of first instance shall require the concurrence of at least four of its members. The court may award the following sentences either singly or in combination:

(a) deprivation of degree or title of degree,
(b) suspension of degree or title of degree,
(c) any sentence considered by them to be lighter than the aforesaid,
(d) deprivation of University office.

(3) Any person sentenced by the Vice-Chancellor and the *Sex Viri* sitting as a court of first instance may within twenty-eight days after notice of their decision lodge an appeal with the Chancellor. Such appeal shall be heard by a court consisting of the Chancellor, or a deputy appointed by him, and two assessors appointed by the Chancellor, all of whom shall be present. The court shall have power by the votes of a majority of all its members to affirm or reverse the decision of the Vice-Chancellor and the *Sex Viri*, or to reduce the sentence.

(4) A court, called the Court of Discipline, shall have jurisdiction over those members of the Colleges and Non-Collegiate Students who are *in statu pupillari*. It shall consist of the Vice-Chancellor and six Heads of Colleges, etc.

S

H.M. JUDGES
AND TRINITY COLLEGE

UNDER an arrangement between the Treasury and the College, H.M. Judge of Assize has a lodging assigned to him in the Master's Lodge of Trinity College. The Judge on his arrival is received in the Great Court by the Master and Fellows and is escorted by them to the dining room of the Lodge, where mulled port is served.

On the day that the Assize begins the Vice-Chancellor, attended by the Bedells and the Yeoman Bedell, and accompanied by the Heads of Houses, the Proctors and other University Officers, proceeds to Trinity Lodge to wait upon the Judge; a sermon is subsequently preached at the University Church by a preacher appointed by the Vice-Chancellor; should the Judge be in Cambridge on a Sunday, he usually attends the University Sermon instead of the special sermon.

THE ADMISSION OF THE NEWLY
ELECTED MASTER OF TRINITY

No ceremony in the University is more picturesque than the admission of a newly elected Master of Trinity College. In Dr Parry's recently published *Memoir* of the late Professor Henry Jackson, a letter is printed giving an account of the installation of the present Master, Sir J. J. Thomson, on 5 March, 1918. "I am glad [said the venerable Professor of Greek] that you thought the ceremonial dramatic. There is an excellent document prepared in 1841—it is said by Welsford (otherwise Mephistopheles) the Chapel Clerk,—which fixes all the details. The V. M. 'commands' the porters to open the Great Gates: then welcomes the M. C. and presents him to the fellows (*not* as the Chronicle says 'presents the fellows to him'). To the Chapel the V. M. takes the right hand, the M. C. designate the left. The V. M. says the formula of admission at the M. C.'s stall, holding his hand. I was glad that the 5th Company of Officer Cadets turned out in force...."

The Fellows assembled in the Ante-Chapel instead of the Combination Room.

The above account is described from the inside. It may be added that Sir Joseph Thomson (who wore his hood squared) was kept waiting outside the closed Gate until his Letters Patent had been formally inspected; and that a large crowd, which had assembled, watched the distinguished man of science as he knocked loudly at the double doors.

COMMEMORATION OF
BENEFACTORS

THE old *Missa pro Benefactoribus*, as copied in Stokes's *Book* in the Registry, carries us back quite early in University history; and the long list of names which are read, or taken as read, at the interesting Service in *Commemoration of Benefactors*, reminds us of the continued liberality of generous donors down the ages. And the splendid procession still marches on.

Royal Benefactors lead the way. A remarkable list of homely but well-to-do worthies, who filled the important post of University Bedells, comes next. Founders of Professorships and Scholarships are remembered. John Crane who provided for the relief of sick scholars, and Henry Latham who started a Pension Fund in connection with University families, are recorded. Benefactors of the Library, of the Schools, of the Museums, of the Laboratories are named. Former Chancellors and University officials are linked with munificent donors of modern times. Prominent names are emphasised, like those of Hugh de Balsham, Sir Richard Whittington, and Sir Isaac Newton.

Altogether some two hundred names are included in this remarkable record.

Several times the lift has been revised, forgotten benefactors being remembered, and new names added. Such additions are continually forthcoming.

THE UNIVERSITY AND
COLLEGE CHESTS

A VERY interesting feature of the University and of the Colleges in early times was the Chests. "The chests... were made of stout oak planks, from two to three inches thick, ... and secured by locks and padlocks with different wards, so as to require the presence of several officials at the same time to open them.... The statutes of nearly every college... enjoin the safe keeping of the chests, the common seal, the valuables (*jocalia*) of the House, the charters, royal letters patent, and other important documents, to which books are not unfrequently added." Some of them were *loan-chests*, where a student deposited some object of value as a *pledge*. Now and then, in the case of manuscripts, a note may be seen, recording the fact that it had been placed in one of the Chests as a pledge.

For these Chests there were Warders and Auditors. In the Grace Books, in connection with the University Chests, there was generally each year a list headed: *Cautiones deliberate novis procuratoribus et jam in cista posite.* "If we take the year 1516, 7 as an example we find deposited in the University Chest 12 spoons, a salt-cellar, a gold signet-ring, a crystal cup (*mirra*), etc." (See the article on the Treasury or Muniment Room in the third volume of Willis and Clark.)

The chief of these Chests were those of Walter Neel, Bishop Bateman, Thomas Beaufort, Duke of Exeter, Richard de Billingford, Cardinal Bourchier, Hugh Fenn, etc. All of the funds connected with the Chests have disappeared; although such ladies as Elizabeth Clere and other benefactors gave sums of money to replenish them.

As for the Chests themselves, some still remain—such as the first old "University Hutch," which still stands in the Registry—and others which are preserved at certain Colleges—such as those in the Treasury at Corpus.

All income accruing to the University is still credited to the account of "the University Chest," over which the University has complete control. The receipts of the Chest—Rents, Fines, Capitation Tax, Fees, etc., together with the Treasury Grant; the common University Fund, provided by contributions levied upon the Colleges; and various special Trusts—these items of University finance make up the academical income.

The University Chest

OBSOLETE OFFICERS

CERTAIN University officers, who formerly held academical poſts of considerable importance, and took part in picturesque funċtions, ought not to be for⁄gotten, in a review of our Ceremonies.

THE MASTER OF GLOMERY

The Maſter of Glomery has had the advantage, or the disadvantage, of coming before us as something of a myſtery. At his entrance in 1276, he is preceded by a mace⁄bearer; at his exit in 1539, he is accompanied by the glamour of the reputation of Sir John Cheke. By the supposed virtues of his office, he looms some⁄what large; but when we meet him in the flesh, he does not seem so important. When Magiſter Glomeriae is named, we are impressed; but we find a rather ordinary person when we are aċtually introduced to Mr Thomas Hunt, or any other member of the liſt given in the *Archdeacon's Book*, or to Mr Begton tendering his rent to Peterhouse, to Mr Abbott paying up arrears to King's, or to Mr Ayera ſtruggling to keep up appear⁄ances in St Katharine's Hoſtel. When our official

ſtands in the chief place on great occasions in the
Senate House, we admire; but the admiration lessens,
when we find his connexion with Grammar is re⁄
garded as a sign of inferiority, and that his position is
really due to a kind of neutrality that makes him a
convenience to rival candidates.

It may be that before the regular inſtitution of the
University, there were certain Grammar Schools, over
the maſters of which the Maſter of Glomery was rector,
and that for a while that official had some position in
affairs academic—as evinced by his bedell and as
shown by a certain jurisdiction assigned to him; but
the bedell had only a narrow sphere and he soon dis⁄
appears altogether; while as to the jurisdiction it is
simply said that he "shall enjoy the same privilege as
the other maſters have with respect to their scholars in
deciding their causes," and naturally (as the old
Statute 36 shows) the jurisdiction of the Regent
Maſters is limited.

Thus does the present writer sum up the former
position of the Maſter of Glomery in a volume on
Mediaeval Hoſtels (C.A.S. vol. XLIX), which contains
a special chapter (no. XIII) on this official. Dean Pea⁄
cock, in his *Observations* has an elaborate article on this
official; he quotes the various Statutes (nos. 4, 54, 62,
117, etc.) which refer to him, he alludes to the cere⁄

monies at the taking of a grammar degree; he quotes
from the *Archdeacon's Book* the *Commissio Glomeriae* and
the *Juramentum*; and he gives part of Bishop Balsham's
Instrument deciding the differences between the powers
of the Archdeacon and the Chancellor as to the
Master of Glomery and the Glomerelli.

The late Professor Skeat said that "*glamorye* or *glo-
marye* is a mere perversion of *gramarie* which is a form
of *gramaire*, 'grammar.'"

THE MASTER IN GRAMMAR

A form of graduation which obtained of old was
that of "Master in Grammar"; though this degree
always ranked lower than that of Arts. The ceremonies at the creation of a "M. Gram.," *ferula et virgis*,
may be quoted from Appendix A, p. xxxvii, of Dean
Peacock's *Proceedings*:

> Whan the Father hath arguyde as shall plese the Proctour, the
> Bedyll in Arte shall bring the Master of Gramer to the Vice chaun-
> celar, delyveryng hym a Palmer wyth a Rodde, whych the Vyce-
> chauncelar shall gyve to the seyde Master in Gramer, & so create
> hym Master. Than shall the Bedell purvay for every master in Gramer
> a shrewde Boy, whom the master in Gramer shall bete openlye in the
> Scolys, & the master in Gramer shall give the Boye a Grote for hys
> Labour, & another Grote to hym that provydeth the Rode and the
> Palmer &c. de singulis. And thus endythe the Acte in that Facultye.

The last record of a degree in grammar refers to

Geoffrey Gethyn in the year 1547-8; see *Grace Book*
Δ, p. 48.

TAXORS

The altered relationship between the University and
the town of Cambridge led to the abolition of the
formerly important office of the Taxors. These two
officers, who were elected with much formality at the
beginning of each academical year, were chosen from
the House of Regents to tax lodging houses and to fix
the assizes of provisions. They were concerned with
the markets and the fairs. The office was abolished in
1856. They had seats next to the Proctors.

Two curious pictures may be seen in the Hare MSS
in the Registry; one showing the destruction of false
measures, etc., by the Taxors, and the other relating
to the homage paid formerly by the Mayor and other
Corporation officials to the University authorities.

SCRUTATORS

Another important office which is now obsolete is
that of the Scrutators, who in the House of non-
Regents corresponded with the Proctors in the House
of Regents. The distinction between the two Houses
disappeared in the new Senate House.

The Taxors

*The Mayor and Corporation paying
homage to the University Authorities*

GAGERS, PRISERS, ETC.

Several minor officers have been abolished, such as the *Gagers,* who tested the "dry" measures, when the University still supervised the markets; the *Prisers,* who valued the goods of deceased members of the University and others.

THE UNIVERSITY
AND STOURBRIDGE FAIR

THE connection between the University and Stourbridge Fair was, of old, very intimate; the academic
authorities claiming great power in the management
and the tolls of the Fair.

In the late Professor John Mayor's *Life of Ambrose
Bonwicke,* there is a characteristic mass of notes illus-
trating this claim (see pp. 153 to 165), including a
summary of the numerous references in Cooper's
Annals. Here may be seen records of the frequent con-
flicts between the town and the University as to their
respective jurisdiction; also various accounts (including Defoe's) of the Fair itself. The proceedings of the
proctors and the taxors are detailed; and how the Vice-
Chancellor and the doctors rode to the Fair, and made
proclamation on horseback. In 1534, the King's Council decreed that "Styrbridge faire was in the suburbes
of Cambridge, and that the Vice-Chancellor or his
commyssary might kepe courte cyvyll ther for plees
wheare a scholar was one party. Item that in the same
faire the university had the oversight, correction and

punyshemente of all weightes and mesures, of all maner of victayll, of all regraters and forestallers," etc.

The "lord of the taps" in his red coat is described; and the sale of books in *Cook's row* is mentioned.

On the one hand we read of Dr Bentley, as Vice-Chancellor in 1701, imprisoning an actor, and ordering the booth built for the theatre to be demolished; on the other hand, later on, we find a vivid description, in Gunning's *Reminiscences,* of Dr Farmer and his "Shakespeare Gang" visiting the Fair.

But Stourbridge Fair and its glories have departed.

THE UNIVERSITY ARMS

THE arms now borne by the University: *gules, on a cross ermine between four lions passant gardant or, a book gules*, were granted by Robert Cooke, Clarencieux King of Arms, on 9 June 1573. Dr Woodham, of Jesus College, published an essay in the first volume of the quarto series of the Cambridge Antiquarian Society on the heraldry of the University, and Mr (afterwards Sir) Wm St John Hope made an elaborate communication to the same Society on 16 November 1892 on the Armorial Ensigns of the University and Colleges (printed in 1894). Sir William said that "although blazoned as *passant* the lions are really *passant gardant, i.e.* lions of England, typical of the royal patronage of the University." Burke and other authorities describe the book as a Bible, but for this there is no warrant.

The *Historical Register* (p. 5) gives the proper blazon of the Arms, speaking of *four gold leopards*.

THE UNIVERSITY MOTTO

THE Elizabethan Statutes (following those of King
Edward VI) begin with the words *Deum timeto: regem
honorato: virtutem colito: disciplinis bonis operam dato*. But
the University gradually adopted as its *motto*, the *em-
blem* first used by John Legate, appointed Printer to
the University in the year 1588. The well-known figure
of *Alma Mater Cantabrigiensis* surrounded by the motto
Hinc Lucem et Pocula Sacra was first used by that printer
in a volume issued in 1600; and has since been em-
ployed in a variety of forms by the University Press.
Michael Drayton, in his *Polyolbion* (1622) has the
following lines, in the twenty-first song:

> O noble Cambridge then, my most beloved town,
> In glory flourish still, to heighten thy renown;
> In woman's perfect shape, still be thy emblem right,
> Whose one hand holds a cup, the other bears a light.

It is usually said that the origin of the motto *Hinc
Lucem et Pocula Sacra* is unknown; but at least it may
be stated that the phrase is frequently quoted by Archbishop Robert Leighton in an expanded form, and

that on one occasion (see his sermon on Psalm xxxii) he gives the translation

Hence light we draw, and fill the sacred cup,

which suggests that the original hexameter ran:

Hinc lucem haurire est *et pocula sacra* replere.

INDEX

Almond, A. G., *Cambridge Robes*, etc., 46
Andrewes, Bp., 47
Annals, Cooper's, 3, 78
Archaeological Journal, 43
Archdeacon, J., Printer, 15
Archdeacon's Book, 73, 75
Ascham, Roger, 58
Ash-Wednesday, 32, 33, 56

Balfour, Earl of, Chancellor, 3
Balsham, Hugh de, Bp., 69, 75
Beaufort, Lady Margaret, 31
Bedells, Esquire, 19–24
Bell, School, 33
Bentley, Dr, Master of Trinity, 38, 79
Beverley, John, v, 1, 7, 21, 24, 55
Bidding Prayer, 54–5
Borlase, George, Registrary, 15
Browne, Dr Thomas, 7
Buck, John, v, 20
Buckingham, Duke of, George Villiers, 21
Bull-dogs, 15
Burghley, Lord, 44, 47
Burwell, 59
Butter-measure, 15
Byron, Lord, 26

Cambridge Cameos, 8, 22, 38
Cambridge Portfolio, 7

Cappa, 39, 44, 45
Caryl, Lynford, Jesus College, 12, 20
C.A.S. Proceedings, 14, 15, 21, 74, 80
Catharine's, St, College, 7
Chain and badge, 23–4
Chancellor, 1–5, 6, 12, 21–24, 40–2, 49, 50, 65, 69, 75
Chancellor's Medals, 5
Chests, 72
Chest, University, 14
Cheke, Sir John, 58, 73
Christ's College, 21, 24, 31
Clare College, 37, 46
Clark, J. W., Registrary, 13, 37, 38
Clark, Prof. E. C., 43, 47
Clere, Alexander, Corpus Christi College, 47
Coke, Sir Edward, 60
Cole, William, antiquary, 20
Colleges, order of Presentation, 30
Comitia majora, 32
Commemoration of Benefactors, 69–70
Commencement, 20, 36–7, 38, 46
Commissary, 63
Congregations, 10, 15, 17, 18, 27, 29, 30, 42

Constables, University, 18
Cooper's *Annals*, 3, 78
Corpus Christi College, 44, 45, 47
Costume, University, 2, 4, 9, 10, 15, 16, 23, 30, 31, 34, 35, 36, 37, 39, 42, 43–8, 51
Country Life, 8, 22, 38
Crane, John, Benefactor, 69
Creation, 34
Croke, Richard, 58
Cromwell, O., 25
Cromwell, Thos., 60
Cup, Essex, 8

Degrees, 28–35
Degrees, Hon., 40–2, 49
Dillon, Lord, 15
Documents, Original, 33
Drayton, Michael, *Polyolbion*, 81
Duckworth, Dr, Jesus College, Senior Proctor, 14, 15
Dukes of Devonshire, Chancellors, 4

Eachard, Dr, 7
Encyclopaedia Britannica, 43, 45
Essex, Earl of, Chancellor, 8, 60
Evans, A. H., Esq. Bedell, 24

Farmer, Dr, Master of Emmanuel, 79
Fisher, Bp. John, Chancellor, 1, 6
Foxe, *Book of Martyrs*, 51
Fuller, Dr Thos., 12

Gagers, 77
Gascoigne, *Theological Dictionary*, 48
Gazeley, S., v
Glomery, Master of, 23, 73–5
Grace-Books, 71, 76
Graces, 27, 28
Grafton, Duke of, Chancellor, 4, 47
Gray, Thomas, 4
Great St Mary's Church, 36, 56, 66
Gunning, Henry, v, vi, 21, 24, 36, 59
Gunning's *Reminiscences*, 36, 59, 79

Haddon, Walter, Master, Trinity Hall, 7
Halberd, Proctors' 14, 15
Hardwicke, Earl of, 60
Hare, ix, 7, 76
Harradine, *Costumes of the University*, 46
Herbert, George, 58
High Steward, 60
Historical Register, vi, 6, 36, 43, 58, 80
Hobbs, Robert, 11, 20
Holland, Earl of, Chancellor, 2
Hope, Sir W. St John, 80
Hubbard, Henry, Emmanuel, Registrary, 23
"Huddling," 32
Hughes, Francis, Esq. Bedell, 20
Humphry, A. P., Esq. Bedell, 21, 24

Huſtler, William, Regiſtrary, 13, 15
Hutton, Dr, Archbp. of York, 33

Insignia, 8, 15
Insignia Doctoralia, 38, 39

Jebb, Sir Richard, 88
Jews, 34–5
Judges of Assize, H.M., 66

Keynes, Dr, Regiſtrary, 13
King's College Chapel, 57

Lamb, Dr, C.C.C., 19, 39
Latham, Henry, Benefactor, 69
Leapingwell, George, 19, 39
Legate, John, Printer, 81
Leighton, Robert, Archbp., 81
Linſtock, Proctor's, 15
Liri-pipe, 45
Loggan, Cantabrigia Illuſtrata, 43
"Lord of the taps," 79
Luard, H. R., Regiſtrary, 13

Maces, 8, 19, 21, 22, 23
Madew, Dr, 7
Maſter of Glomery, 23
Maſter in Grammar, 75–6
Matriculation, 25–6
Mawson, Dr, 38
Mayor, Prof. John, 78
Medals, Chancellors', 5
Mere, John, 8, 33, 57
Monmouth, Duke of, Chan-
cellor, 23

More, Sir Thomas, 60
Moule, Charles, 58
Mullinger, Dr, University His-
tory, 54
Music Odes, 37
Music Speeches, 37

Newcaſtle, Duke of, Chan-
cellor, 23
Newton, Sir Isaac, 69
Nichols's Progresses, 55
Northumberland, Duke of,
Chancellor, 5

Observations, etc., 20, 32, 38
Obsolete Officers, 23, 73–7
Orationes et Epiſtolae Canta-
brigienses, 58
Orator, see Public Orator
Ordinances, 27

Partisan, Proctors', 15
Peacock, Dean, v, 20. 32, 38,
51, 74, 75
Pearce, Dr E. C., Maſter of
C.C.C., v
Peile, Dr John, 4
Pelzer, John, Epiſtolae Obscu-
rorum Virorum, 47
Pemberton, W. A., Regiſtrary,
15
Perne, Dr, 55
Pitt, William, 60
Praelectors, 30
Presentation of Address, 53
Prevaricator, 32
Prince Consort, Chancellor, 4

Prisers, 77
Processions, 50–2
Proctors, 14
Pro-Proctors, 16
Public Orator, 40, 41, 50, 58, 59

Randall, Dr, 4
Rashdall, Dean, *Universities*, 39
Rawlinson, J. F. P., M.P., 63
Rayleigh, Lord, Chancellor, 23
Redfern, W. B., 15
Regalia, 7
Registrary, The, 11, 12, 13, 40, 52
Registry, 7, 69, 72
Representation in Parliament, 61
Ridley, Bp., Nicholas, Proctor, 20
Robinson, H. F., 47
Romilly, Joseph, Registrary, 13, 15

Salisbury, Earl of, 60
Sandys, Sir John, 38, 39, 58
Schonfeld, Dr V., *The Real Jew*, 47, 48
Scrutators, 76
Seal, University, 7, 8
Senate House, 4, 5, 17, 18, 32, 39, 40–2, 58, 74
Senate House Yard, 40, 50
Seward, Dr, Master of Downing, v
Sex Viri, 64–5
Shipley, Sir A., Master of Christ's, v, 8, 21, 22, 37, 38
Skeat, Prof., 75
Smith, Sir Thomas, 58

Stanford, Sir C. V., 5
Stanley, Dr, V.-C., 7
Statuta Academiae Cantabrigiensis, 15
Statutes, New, 1–6, 8, 25, 49
Statutes University, 20, 25, 44, 74, 81
St Benet's Church, 57
St Botolph's Church, 57
St Catharine's College, 7
Stokes, H. P., *Esquire Bedells*, 51, 52
—— *Mediaeval Hostels*, 74
Stokes, Matthew, v, 11, 12, 51, 57, 69
Stourbridge Fair, 44, 78, 79
Stratford, John de, Archbp. of Canterbury, 44
Supplicats, 28, 30

Tabor, James, 12
Tanner, Dr, vi, 6, 14, 36, 43, 58
Taxors, 76
Townsend, John, of Norfolk, 15
Trinity College, 66–8
—— Master of, Admission, 66
Trinity Hall, 16
Tripos, 29, 32–35

University Arms, 80
—— Calendar, 34
—— Chest, 14, 71, 72
—— Church, 16
—— Constables, 18
—— Costume, 43–8, and *see* Costume

University Discipline, 64, 65
—— Marshall, 23
—— Motto, 81
—— Seal, 8
—— Sermons, 56, 57
University Society in the Eighteenth Century, 36

Venn, Dr, 25
Vice-Chancellor, *passim*

Wall, Adam, v, 21
Walmisley, Prof., 4
Whitgift, Dr, Archbp. of Canterbury, 33
Whittington, Sir Richard, Benefactor, 69

Willis and Clark, *Architectural History*, 72
Wood, Anthony, 44
Wooden Spoon, 31
Woodham, Dr, Jesus College, 80
Wordsworth, Christopher, Public Orator, 58
Wordsworth, Christopher, *University Society*, etc., 36
Wordsworth, William, 4
Worts, William, Esquire Bedell, 23
Wrangler, Senior, 31

Yeoman Bedell, 22, 23
York, Duke of, 14

Milton Keynes UK
Ingram Content Group UK Ltd.
UKHW010852110324
439075UK00008B/52